AROUND LONDON

Front cover picture:
Ludgate Hill and Circus 1897 (L130037)

Above:
South Street, Romford 1908 (59808)

FRANCIS FRITH AND HIS
UNIQUE ARCHIVE

In 1860, Francis Frith, the Quaker son of a Chesterfield cooper, was 38 years old. He had already sold a massive grocery business he had built up, for a small fortune. Like Livingstone and Stanley, Frith was fired with a romantic Wanderlust, and the Victorian deep passion for travelling and exploring. Between 1857 and '59 he made several pioneering photographic journeys to remote regions of the Nile that brought him considerable fame.

After his marriage in 1860, he confined his wanderings a little closer to home and began a series of photo trips around Britain. His aim was to make his pictures available to the greatest number of people possible - life was hard and drab for millions of Victorians, and Frith believed his 'view souvenirs' of seaside resorts, beauty spots and town and village scenes would help keep their rare days out alive in their memories. He was right: by 1890 he had created the largest photographic publishing company in the world!

As well as thousands of views of high streets around Britain, Frith's growing archive included beautiful scenes of leafy glades, dusty lanes, rocks and coastlines, and the boats and riversides, beloved of Victorian wanderers like Jerome K Jerome - whose 'Three Men in a Boat' had struck a strong chord with the public.

Life in the Frith family was never dull. The family went with him on many trips, and the highlights were recorded by his wife, Mary Ann, in her journal. In 1872 she tells of a relaxing three week expedition to Ilfracombe in North Devon. Whilst such trips may have been something of a holiday for his wife and children, Francis Frith found no time to put his feet up. He was up and down the coast photographing Barnstaple and Lynton, hiring carters to carry him out to remote locations, and boatsmen to row him round the bay to view and photograph spectacular cliff formations.

After Francis Frith died in 1898 his sons carried on the business for many years with great success, specialising in postcards and other prints. So impressive is the archive he started that **The Financial Times** called it '*a unique and priceless record of English life in the last century*'.

AROUND LONDON

A Century of Change

This edition published by
The Francis Frith Collection exclusively for
Selectabook Ltd., Roundway, Devizes,
Wiltshire SN10 2HR

Picture compilation and text by Jenny de Gex and
Terry Sackett
Designed by Terry Sackett

First Published in 1996

© The Francis Frith Collection

ISBN 1 85937 025 X

Printed in Italy by Imago Publishing

The Francis Frith Collection
The Old Rectory, Bimport, Shaftesbury, Dorset SP7 8AT
Tel: 01747 855669 Fax: 01747 855065

CONTENTS

HAMPSTEAD. Once a renowned spa, this handsome, old London village is set on the slopes of the hill that leads up to the famous Heath. With its narrow passages and courts and promenades shaded with limes, it still retains its charming village atmosphere. Here lived the fashionable, the wealthy and the great, who joined the throngs of Londoners strolling leisurely up to Whitestone Hill to enjoy the bracing air and fine panoramas of the City of London far below. On clear, sunny days they could pick out Windsor Castle, the hills of Hertfordshire and the heathlands of Surrey.

Top: North End, Hampstead 1898 (41579) Described as 'the place of groves', Hampstead was always a popular residential area. Its many notable inhabitants in the 19th century included Byron and Keats, Robert Louis Stevenson and the painter John Constable, whose many skyscapes and views of the Heath are testament to its then rural location. **Above: Spaniards Road, Hampstead Heath 1898** (41595) More like a country lane than the main road it is today, this road crossing the Heath affords panoramic views over London's skyline below. In the 16th century a beacon was built on the hill to warn if the Spanish Armada had landed, and in the 19th century the first Admiralty semaphore telegraph was constructed there.

Above: The Spaniards, Hampstead 1890 (L130095) Said to have been named after a Spanish Ambassador to the court of King James I, this pub played its part in history when the Gordon Rioters were plied by so much drink by the landlord, that by the time guards arrived to arrest them, they were completely drunk. Dickens regularly visited 'The Spaniards', which provided the setting for some of his scenes.

Left: The Bull and Bush, Hampstead 1898 (41581) Hampstead was always popular with poets and writers: Pope and his friends met at the Upper Flask in East Heath Road. Keats and Shelley were frequent later visitors to the neighbourhood's taverns.

Above: Vale of Health, Hampstead 1898 (41588) Water was most important to the history of Hampstead. Spring water with reputed medicinal properties was discovered in 1698, on what is now Well Walk. By 1700 spring water 'of the same nature and equal in virtue with Tunbridge Wells' was being sold in London's taverns for 3d a flask. A fashionable pump room was built soon after.

Left: Viaduct and Pond, Hampstead 1898 (41587) The City was authorised to convey water from the springs to the rest of London. However, some of the water came from 'a large pond in the Vale of Health, full of weeds, swarming with animal life...' according to Hassall's 1850s *Microscopic Examination of the Water Supplied to the Inhabitants of London.*

Opposite above: St Stephen's from Pond, Hampstead 1898 (41589)

Opposite below: Bathing Pond, Hampstead 1898 (41590)

Above: Hampstead Heath from Parliament Hill 1890 (41600)
It is strange to think the heath was once roamed by deer, wolves, and wild boar. Densely forested thousands of years ago, by the late 17th century most of the forest had been cleared for timber needed to rebuild London after the Great Fire. The Heath was finally saved for the public in 1871. Fairs are still held there at Easter and Bank Holidays.

Left: Whitestone Pond, Hampstead 1898 (41592) An old white milestone, after which Whitestone Pond is named, announces that the place is 'IV miles from St Giles Pound and 4½ miles 29 yards from Holborn Bars'.

Opposite: High Street, Hampstead 1898 (41570) Although most of the street-level premises are now shops, many of the 18th-century buildings have been preserved.

ARROW ON THE HILL, with its world famous public school, is an ancient settlement of the Saxons, who chose it for the defensive opportunities offered by its steep slopes overlooking the dense woodland in the vale below. The town boasts many fine 17th and 18th century buildings, including Flambards House. Yet, the coming of the Metropolitan Railway wrought great changes, attracting commuters in their thousands. Inevitably, houses quickly smothered the open slopes of the hill.

Right: Harrow on the Hill 1906 (53629) There are fine views of several counties from this lofty summit, the highest in Middlesex. In the centre of the picture, ranging along the edges of the steep slopes, are lines of terraces and villas, built to house the town's increasing commuter population.

Above: Station Road, Harrow on the Hill 1914 (66820) This classic scene depicts changes typical of the Victorian era: a smart new shopping parade and the relentless intrusion of the chain store. On the left is Home & Colonial, and further along the parade, Boots 'the largest chemist in the world' and Sainsbury's. Eastman & Son's delivery bicycle is parked outside their shop, which is on the extreme left.

Above: High Street, Harrow on the Hill 1905 (53630) This peaceful scene is very little changed today. In the background is the soaring spire of St Mary's Church, which is set on the crest of the hill. The hardware shop on the left is offering canary cages - captive singing birds were immensely popular with the Victorians and Edwardians - as well as a wide variety of watering cans, garden rollers and fencing. The Harrow Gazette offices are at the extreme left.

Left: High Street, Harrow on the Hill 1905 (53631) This historic street winds it way down the hill. On the right is the King's Head, dating from 1553, its old carved wooden sign set firmly on the green outside, to attract every approaching carriage and coach.

Above: The Village, Stanmore 1906 (55690) This quiet village scene shows how so much of the fringes of London's countryside must have looked before the onset of the car. On the right is The Fountain Inn, with a horse and cart drawn up in front. The driver is doubtless enjoying a glass of ale inside. He is selling muslin and lace curtains.

Left: The Old Church, Stanmore c1965 (S180070)

Opposite above: The Harrow Schools 1906 (53638). This world famous public school was founded by John Lyon in 1572, originally for the education of local children. Many famous Britons have trodden its corridors, including Lord Byron and Winston Churchill.

Opposite below: The Harrow Schools 'Bill' 1914 (66815) Scholars, immaculate in blazers and boaters, trek between classes.

CHINGFORD. This enormous residential suburb was described in the Victorian era as 'being so agreeably situated for retirement that the most remote distance from the metropolis could hardly excel it'. The Bourne river winds its way round Chingford's eastern edge bound for Highams Park, and on to join the waters of the Lea.

Previous pages: Station Road, Chingford 1907 (58250)

Right: The Royal Forest Hotel, Chingford 1903 (50613) This imposing Tudor-style building sits close by Epping Forest.

Below: Chingford 1906 (55341) A No 4 tram, plastered with advertising signboards for Everett's Tea, thunders its way along the mud-encrusted street bound for Lea Bridge Road. On the right, carrier's horses enjoy a welcome rest from hauling their heavy load of flour sacks.

Top: Station Road, Chingford 1923 (73934) Out of sight beyond the end of this busy street are the peaceful glades of Epping Forest and Queen Elizabeth's Hunting Lodge. The railway came to Chingford in 1873, and it was here that trains from London reached their final destination. On the right W J May & Son's fruiterer's cart is drawn up in front of the shop. **Above: The Owl Inn, Lippitt's Hill, Chingford c1900** (50612) Close by Aldergrove Wood, this handsome inn with its long timber slats was typical of the weatherboarded style of this woodland region. It was demolished in the 1960s. A cart, piled high with baskets, stands outside.

WOODFORD is the principal suburb bordering Epping Forest. In the 17th century there were 60,000 acres remaining of this huge vastness of woods and grassy plains, and the last surviving part of the even greater Royal Forest of Essex that stretched from Romford across to the River Lea. For centuries Londoners had slashed and cut at the thick woodland, making clearings, building cottages and grazing their animals. From the late 19th century onwards, the pace of encroachment quickened, until between the wars, in our own century, small settlements like Woodford had grown into sprawling suburbs.

Right: High Road, Woodford 1921 (70105) The town marches on into the ancient forest. A few old trees survive as a sad reminder of its original glory. But the invasion was inevitable - London's growing population had to be housed. On the left is the George Hotel. Men cycle to work along the broad, shaded highway.

Above: High Street, Woodford 1903 (50604) This great conurbation extends eastwards to the Chigwell Road. On the left is The Castle, an Ind Coope house. It was the major local brewer, with its brewery close by in neighbouring Romford. Just beyond is a painted sign advertising 'Broome's Horses Corn Cure'. **Opposite page: George Lane, Woodford 1921** (70095) A winding street of Victorian terraces. There are no cars in sight, and a cyclist and a mother and pram dawdle in the middle of the road without a care.

Above: Salway Hill, Woodford Green 1921 (70109) A street of Victorian villas in a rich variety of styles, built to house the growing number of City commuters who flocked here to live during the last century.

Left: Woodford Green 1904 (53059) It is hard to believe that this bustling suburb was once a peaceful village surrounded by the cool, green groves of Epping Forest. Here we see one the rickyard of one of the many local farms.

Opposite above: Wood Street Station, Walthamstow 1907 (58548B) The Great Eastern Railway crosses the street here, offering rapid journeys to the City of London.

Opposite below: St James Street, Walthamstow 1906 (55200) A handcart threads its way fearlessly through thick traffic, carefully negotiating the tram tracks. On the right, Everett's Stores are offering their own brand tea for 1/6d.

Right: Hale End Cottages, Walthamstow 1904 (51423) Simple cottages, like those shown here, have been built down the centuries by fiercely independent yeoman farmers in clearings in the Royal Forest of Waltham. The Midland Railway brought massive changes in the 19th century, and soon the region became the home of a very different breed of people - City clerks and shop workers.

Below: The Public Baths, Walthamstow 1904 (51525) Public hygiene was a preoccupation of Victorian social engineers, who believed that good health and cleanliness were vital elements in a civilised society for the creation of a stable, contented and productive workforce. Public baths sprang up all over London during Victoria's reign.

Above: Forest Road, Wathamstow 1909
(62070a) In the centre is The Bell Inn, an ornate confection of Victorian brick and faience. On the left is a newspaper hoarding announcing a special report on 'Matt Wells's Blunder'. What could he have done?

Left: Chapel End, Walthamstow c1890
(51424) An old-style policeman on the beat impresses local children with his authority. The simple one-storey wooden dwelling behind the picket fence blends perfectly with the tree-lined street.

ROMFORD. The town we see today is choked with a jungle of suburbs and cut to shreds by traffic. Yet it was once a major market centre for the countryside around, with weekly cattle, hog and corn markets. As is so often the case, it was the coming of the railway that changed the face of Romford for ever, bringing manufacturing businesses to the town, including the world famous brewer, Ind Coope.

Right: High Street, Romford 1908 (59807) Rich in old houses, some timber-lapped and many-gabled, the High Street winds round towards the spacious Market Place. Young girls in broad hats and bright white pinafore dresses pose for the camera. On the left is the Jubilee Coffee Tavern, and on the right Borrow's the Fish and Potato Merchant.

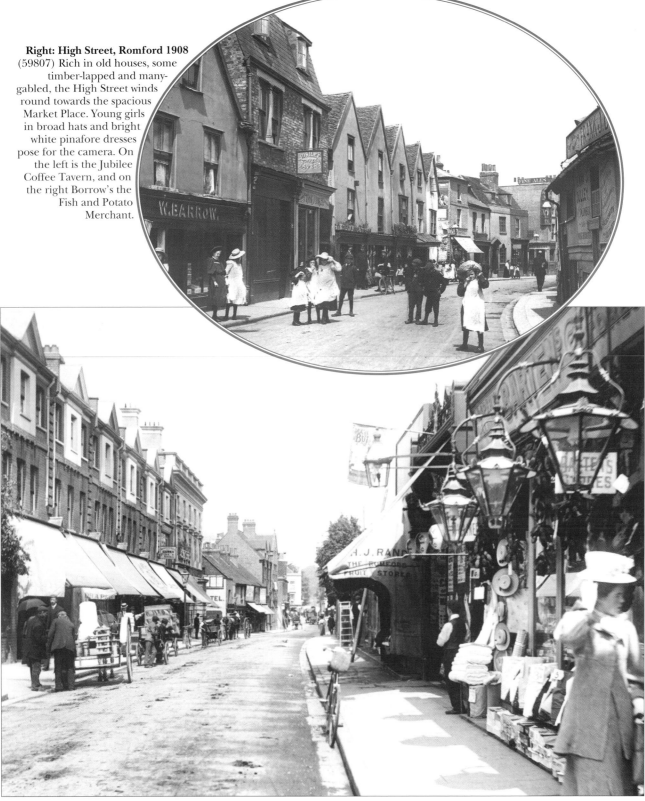

Above: South Street, Romford 1908 (59808) This charming scene shows town life as it must have been in old Romford. The street is packed tight with small shops, their displays tumbling out over the pavement. On the right is Barten's Cash Stores, offering bolts of cloth, straw hats, jackets, shoes and matting. Note its ornate gas lamps. On the left, an old man is unloading milk pails from his cart.

Above: The Ind Coope Brewery, Romford 1908 (59827A) This massive brewery complex relied heavily on the railway for transportation throughout the country. In the middle of the picture, barrels of beer are stacked in their hundreds, ready to be loaded onto rail trucks. Note the efficient-looking vegetable plot in the foreground.

Left: The Railway Station, Romford 1908 (59826) Elegant ladies in fashionable hats adorned with feathers and foliage await the steam train. Fast travel on the Great Eastern encouraged the growth of Romford's suburbs like Gidea Park.

Overleaf: Romford Market 1910 (62770) A bustling market scene that has changed little in essence since Henry III's time, when the town's Market Charter was granted. The broad square is filled to bursting with animal pens, and canny farmers from the surrounding villages eye up the cattle that are to be auctioned. In the background is the Victorian church of St Edward's.

Above: The Windmill, Hornchurch 1909 (62085) The Hornchurch Mill's cart is loading up with sacks of flour.

Left: High Road, Chadwell Heath 1908 (60606)

Opposite top: High Street, Hornchurch 1909 (62081) On the right of this tranquil village scene is the tile-clad Bull Inn, since demolished and replaced with a fake half-timbered building. Franklyn the butcher, on the left, is a purveyor of home-killed English meat, and has a display of cuts in the street outside hanging from hooks that would be a modern health inspector's nightmare!

Opposite below: The Village, Hornchurch 1908 (59856) Here we see some charming old weatherboarded houses that depict the essence of Essex vernacular architecture. The carter is grooming his horses ready for the road.

PMINSTER.
Although it is now criss-crossed by traffic-clogged highways, Upminster has a long and historic heritage, and boasts many outstanding old buildings, including Upminster Hall, which dates back to the 15th century. There is a famous smock mill, a 17th-century red brick Clock House, and an ancient tithe barn established by the monks of Waltham Abbey. Despite its modern expansion, Upminster still has the atmosphere of a pleasant garden suburb.

Top: The Mill, Upminster 1908 (59867) This handsome smock mill was built in 1803 by James Noakes, and was in use until the 1930s. The miller stands outside posing formally for the camera. Its huge sails did not provide the motive power for long - a steam engine was installed in 1811 to grind the corn. **Above: Broadway, Upminster 1908** (60613) James Matthews' coal waggon pauses outside the Bell Hotel. The elegant grey horse takes a welcome breather. The local postboy leans nonchalantly against the wheel. It looks as if the solid brick-built hotel is up for sale - Woodman & Sons of Romford, brokers and valuers, have their signboard showing on the right.

Above: The Market, Upminster 1908
(60612) This view shows a new parade of shops built to serve the needs of the many commuters who swelled the local population after the railway arrived. On the left is Searson's Emporium offering bargain-priced shoes. Futher along, Mrs Talbot peeps out of the doorway of her fruiterer's shop. A boy is looking after his younger brothers and sisters, including the tiny baby in the pram.

Left: Birds Lane Corner, Upminster 1909 (62095) One would never believe that traffic on the main Southend arterial highway now hurtles across this peaceful lane with its simple timber cottages. Great trees shade the party of walkers. Across the fields are farms and pockets of woodland. Set at the outer fringes of London, Upminster still has its quiet corners.

CENTRAL LONDON. The Romans colonised a flourishing trading city in about AD 43-50 and named it Londinium. On the shores of the Thames and in the City, proof of the earliest settlement has been found, including the remains of London Wall, which can be clearly seen in several places, which surrounded the city with six main gates. Today the City flourishes in a different way, trading internationally in a new technological world, nonetheless based on the history of the medieval merchants and their traditional Livery Companies and Guilds, and the power of Britain's former Empire.

Right: The Tower of London c1920 (L130251) The Tower was begun by William the Conqueror soon after the Battle of Hastings in 1066 and added to by successive monarchs. Telling an often bloody history, it has at various times housed the royal armouries, the mint and observatory, the royal menagerie, and still houses one of London's prime tourist attractions, the Crown Jewels.

Above: Mansion House and Cheapside 1890 (L130209) The Mansion House is the official residence of the Lord Mayor for his or her time in office, and the setting for elaborate City Dinners. **Opposite: Ludgate Hill and Circus 1897** (L130037) Like other city gates, Lud Gate (named in 66 BC after Kind Lud and probably erected by the Romans) was demolished in 1760. Looking towards Wren's masterpiece, St Paul's Cathedral, this busy Fleet Street scene shows the railway that daily brought increasing numbers of workers into the City. **Previous pages: Bank of England and Royal Exchange 1910** (L130207)

Right: Trafalgar Square 1890
(L130133) At the very core of
London, the playing fountains of
Trafalgar Square are a magnet for
tourists even today, who photograph
each other amid a sea of pigeons.
The church of St Martin-in-the-
Fields, behind, stands on the site of
a 12th-century chapel. Eminent
people buried here include Nell
Gwynne, the artists Hogarth and
Reynolds and Chippendale. The
crypt was used to shelter homeless
soldiers returning from the First
World War, and took a direct hit in
the Second, but is now restored as a
restaurant.

Above: Whitehall Horse Guards c1920 (L130423) The daily Changing of the Guard here at Horse Guards and also at Buckingham
Palace are high on London visitors' lists of things to see, as they represent the air of pageantry and tradition that speaks volumes about
British history. The entrance to Horse Guards is virtually unchanged from the 18th-century building designed by William Kent. Only
members of the Royal Family may drive through the central arch.

Above: Trafalgar Square 1908 (L130152) Nelson's column towers 145 foot above the square; the bronze capital decorated with reliefs representing Nelson's battles is cast from old guns from Woolwich Arsenal. Nelson himself is 17 foot high, and a prime target for passing pigeons.

Left: The Strand 1908 (L130165) Looking down the Strand towards St Clement Dane's Church, redesigned by Sir Christopher Wren after the Great Fire and now the central church of the RAF after an equally great fire, the Blitz of 1941. On the left is the Gaiety Theatre, a landmark of Edwardian and 1920s musical theatre, which was demolished in the 1950s.

Right: Piccadilly Circus 1890s
(L130038) The statue of Eros was never intended to represent the God of Love, as we understand it to be today, but instead, the Angel of Christian Charity, after a benevolent Victorian philanthropist, the 7th Earl of Shaftesbury. As it was unveiled by the Duke of Westminster in 1893, the Duchess drank a cup of water from the fountain.

Below: Piccadilly Circus 1886 (L130186) The Circus was originally formed of curved stucco buildings on the corners forming a circle, at the junction of Piccadilly and Nash's Regent Street. When the buildings on the north-eastern end were demolished to form Shaftesbury Avenue in 1880, they were replaced with the London Pavilion, whose outer shell stands today. The inside has been altered beyond all recognition and soon will become a centre for 'virtual reality' computer games.

Top: Regent Street c1890 (L130079) The Regency architect John Nash, who also designed the dignified buildings around Regent's Park, had a scheme to connect this to the Regents' palace, Carlton House. The street we know today was the result. The curved portion known as the Quadrant was to be devoted to shops 'of fashion and taste' and was at the centre of fashion during Victorian times. **Above: Regent Circus 1890** (L130206) Traffic congestion in an increasingly crowded West End cannot have been helped by the odd street musician wheeling along his piano-organ to play to shoppers on their day out.

Above: Cheyne Walk 1890 (L130087)
Taking its name from the Cheyne family,
lords of the manor from 1660-1712,
Cheyne Walk has many beautiful Queen
Anne and later houses, and borders the
River Thames. Many artists and writers
have lived here, including George Eliot,
Carlyle and Rossetti. The latter kept a
menagerie which disturbed the
neighbours, resulting in a clause in leases
forbidding the keeping of peacocks.

Left: Chelsea Embankment 1890
(L130083) The old Thames sailing barges
were very distinctive but are a rare sight
today. Bringing fruit, vegetables or
building materials from Kent and Essex,
some of their most valuable cargoes were
hay and straw for the horses who provided
essential transport on land. The resulting
manure was transported back again to
fertilize the fields.

Top: High Street, Kensington 1893 (K9300) Before the High Street was widened in 1902, it was easy enough to wheel one's perambulator to and from Kensington Gardens, where nannies would sit in rows keeping an eye on their offspring. Queen Victoria spent her youth at Kensington Palace, hence it became the Royal Borough of Kensington, subsequently merged with Chelsea. Frank Giles Upholsterers was there from 1889-1899, next to a pub called 'The Goat' still there today, opposite the Royal Garden Hotel.
Above: High Street, Kensington 1899 (K9024)

Right: Hyde Park Corner c1920
(L139238) The grandiose entrance
to Hyde Park was designed by
Decimus Burton in the 1820s. The
park was originally Henry VIII's deer
park, but became London's largest
park from the 17th century. A toll
gate here had been the main
entrance to London from the West.
Cars are freely using the central arch
which now is only used by
emergency services, the Household
Cavalry or the Royal Family.

Below: Hyde Park 1890 (L130105)
Riding in Hyde Park became a
fashionable pastime, whether on
horseback or in horse-drawn
carriages. A parade to see and be
seen in, it was part of an active social
season, from the 17th century
onwards. Coachmen wore smart
livery and took enormous pride in
the upkeep of their horses and
vehicles.

Above: Palace and Bridge, Lambeth c1900
(L130139) Paddle steamers such as this
took passengers up and down the Thames
on pleasure cruises and sightseeing trips,
as the view from the river was - and still is -
one of the best ways to see the city.
Lambeth Palace, behind, is the official
residence of the Archbishop of
Canterbury.

Left: Zoological Gardens, 1913 (65252)
Founded in 1826, the Zoological Society
housed its collection of animals from
1828 in Regent's Park, in an area laid out
by Decimus Burton. Bears, monkeys,
kangaroos and the like attracted 30,000
visitors within the first seven months.
Ladies had to be restrained from poking
their parasols through the bars. In 1830
the royal menagerie from Windsor, and in
1832-4 the collection from the Tower of
London, were transferred here. At the
forefront of research and conservation,
and with many 'firsts' both in animals and
buildings, it became commonly known as
the zoo, after a music-hall song.

Above: London Bridge c1900 (L130317) The London Bridge in this photograph now stands in Arizona, transported brick by brick in the late 1960s when it was replaced. The first bridge was made of wood during the Roman occupation, and the first stone bridge built in the 12th century. The variety of transport shown here includes 'growlers', hansom cabs and carriers' carts.

Left: St Paul's 1890 (L130126) Seen from the south bank of the Thames, not far from the original site of Shakespeare's Globe Theatre, St Paul's dominates the skyline.

Opposite top: Tower Bridge 1895 (L130168) Opened by the Prince of Wales in 1884 with great processions and ceremony, Tower Bridge has a unique hydraulic drawbridge.

Opposite below: Houses of Parliament 1908 (L130149) These Gothic-style buildings were created by Sir Charles Barry and Augustus Pugin following the 1834 fire of the Palace of Westminster.

Above: Houses of Parliament 1890 (L130162)
Wordsworth wrote enthusiastically of a
sparkling morning in London while standing
on Westminster Bridge: 'Earth has not
anything to show more fair...'

Left: Westminster Abbey c1867 (L130142)
William the Conqueror was crowned in the
Abbey in 1066, the first in a long line of royal
coronations here. Henry III began rebuilding
in the 13th century: subsequent monarchs
made alterations and improvements, notably
Henry VII whose fan-vaulted chapel is a
masterpiece of Tudor building.

Opposite: Parliament Square 1890 (L130008)
Big Ben was originally only the name of the
clock but now means the tower as well. The bell
alone weighed nearly fourteen tons and was
towed through the streets by sixteen horses.
Until automatic winding-gear was installed, it
took two men thirty-two hours to wind the
clock.

Overleaf: St Giles's Circus c1910 (L130218)

AFTERNOON TEA
Tea Rooms J.P. Restaurants Ltd Tea Rooms
TAILORS
FURS
TEAS
TEAS
SHEPHERDS BUSH
WARS 'WHITE LABEL'
WILLESD
DEW
ENERAL
STOUT BLOGG'S BREWERY Ltd

Above: High Street, Foot's Cray 1900
(45834) Set close by the leafy suburbs
of Chislehurst and Sidcup, Foot's Cray
was once little more than a modest
village until the huge changes
wrought during the Victorian era. For
centuries this attractive narrow, dusty
street was a quiet haven, graced by
many fine old buildings. Then
industries sprung up, the turnpike
brought increased traffic, and there
was much new building. On the right
is Thwaites' lovely old weatherboarded
wines and spirits premises. Just beyond
is a new development of Victorian
gabled tile-hung houses. The local
children have turned out for the Frith
photographer.

Left: Foot's Cray Lane 1900
(45835) The main Sidcup to Bexley
railway crosses this placid leafy lane.

ROMLEY is an old market town set on a hill. Despite the inevitable rash of building in recent years, it still retains many fascinating features from its long history. There is the former palace of the Bishop of Rochester set just above the railway, as well as several green recreational areas including Queen's Gardens. Close by were the Victorian pleasure grounds of Crystal Palace, where Londoners flocked for a taste of a fantasy world, far removed from the daily grind of earning a living.

Right: The Parish Church, Bromley 1899 (42938) The old parish church of St Peter & St Paul was almost entirely destroyed during an air raid in 1941. Only the tower and the floor remain. The handsome lych-gate is almost smothered by the overhanging branches of a churchyard tree. Dr Johnson's wife is buried here.

Above: High Street, Bromley 1899 (42935) Aberdeen Buildings, this prestigious parade of shops, was built in 1887. Similar developments were springing up all over London, as the new chainstores competed for the poor man's wages. The tills chimed merrily until late, and gone were the open sacks of flour and tea. Everything was pre-packed, much of it imported from overseas. There were exceptions though: on the right, the man in the striped apron is selling local ducks and fowls.

Above: Ye Old Woode House, Beckenham 1899 (43376) This lovely old building, with its curious central arched beams, housed three different businesses - a sweet shop, a watchmaker and jeweller, and a laundry. You could have your shirts cleaned for 4d, collars and cuffs for 1d, and waistcoats for 5d. The building was demolished in 1920.

Left: Church Hill, Beckenham 1899 (43377)

Opposite top: Bromley 1904 (51892) A horse and trap clatters easily along this peaceful street past the Jolly Farmer. It is a hot summer's day, and the long cooling shadows cast by the buildings stretch indolently out across the street.

Opposite below: View from Recreation Ground, Bromley 1899 (42940) The broad open spaces of the recreation ground offered the people of Bromley welcome relief from the pressures of London life.

Overleaf: The Abbey Schools, Beckenham 1899 (43385)

DULWICH was originally a tiny village set among farms and thick woodland. Almost unique amongst London boroughs, it still hangs on to its rural atmosphere. In the 18th century a spa was established in its park, and it became popular with the early Victorians, who flocked to take its waters.

Right: Dulwich College 1898 (42659) This august college has a long and varied history. It was set up in the reign of James I by the actor Edward Alleyn, and offered education to the poor boys of the village. Alleyn had made his fortune issuing licences for bear and dog baiting. The bulk of the buildings we see today are the work of Charles Barry the Younger and were built in the 1870s.

Below: The Toll Gate, Dulwich 1898 (42658) This is the last surviving toll gate in London. Drovers had to fork out 2½d for 'Sheep, Lambs or Hogs per score' to get through.

Above: High Street, Sydenham 1898
(42670) Originally a remote region of forest and common land, Sydenham became a fashionable residential area for the wealthy during the era when the delights of Crystal Palace were at their most popular. Villas sprung up along the breezy, tree-fringed streets and carriages rattled to and from the City. On the left is Mr Attwood's plumbing and decorating business, with some splendidly ornate signwriting down the side wall. He was doubtless delighted at all the extra work he gained in the houses of the well-heeled and famous.

Left: Sydenham Hill 1889 (42669) Close by were the fantastic glass pleasure domes of Crystal Palace. A family group pauses at a drinking trough during their long climb up the hill. Another traveller has scooped up some refreshing water with a ladle.

CRYSTAL PALACE. The extraordinary glass conservatory known as Crystal Palace was built to house the Great Exhibition in Hyde Park in 1851. Joseph Paxton, the superintendent of the Duke of Devonshire's gardens at Chatsworth, based his designs on a similar conservatory there, and published his drawings in the Illustrated London News. After the Exhibition, it was removed and re-erected across the river at Sydenham, becoming for 80 years the central feature of an amusement park, which sadly ended when the building was completely destroyed by fire in 1936.

Right: The Park, Crystal Palace 1890 (L130021) Crystal Palace Park covers almost 200 acres of gardens and boating lakes, with strange sculptures of prehistoric monsters that still survive today. Crowds flocked to watch any entertainment in the gardens, such as this launch of a hot air balloon, invented in the late 18th century.

Above: The Fountains, Crystal Palace c1890 (C207977) The pleasure gardens boasted formal gardens complete with statues and dancing fountains, fed by two 300 foot water towers. Annual firework displays, known as Brock's Benefits, after the firework manufacturers who supplied them, were held in the Park and gardens.

Top: Crystal Palace c 1886 (C207992) The interior of the Palace was divided into courts and was used as a theatre, concert hall and exhibition space. The construction used 400 tons of glass, 4,000 tons of iron with 200 miles of sash bars and 30 miles of guttering, and employed 2,000 workmen. Temporary exhibitions were held there on an often grand scale. **Above: Crystal Palace c1886** (C207990) and **Overleaf: Crystal Palace 1890** (C207020)

Right: Devonshire Road, Forest Hill 1898 (42673) This bustling residential suburb, now bisected by the busy South Circular road, was once wild forest, bordering Westwood Common and the Great North Wood. The Forest Hill Meat Market is advertising fresh consignments of New Zealand lamb 'at moderate prices'. This was a sign of the times - British farmers had fought a long and fruitless battle against cheap imports for many years.

Below: Upper Norwood c1900 (U42064) The people of this London suburb enjoy a rare display of pomp and pageant, as the Ancient Order of Foresters parade through the town's streets. Note the rider on a horse in cavalier's garb and the banners behind topped with deer antlers. This ceremony underlines Norwood's historic links with the forest and with woodland occupations.

Opposite: Westow Hill, Norwood 1898 (42645) In the distance is one of the 282 foot twin towers of Crystal Palace, wafting black smoke into the South London skies.

Above: The Town Hall, Battersea 1899 (44033)

Left: The Grammar School, Battersea 1900 (44044)

Opposite top: Brockwell Park, near Brixton 1899 (43581) This leafy and expansive green space was opened to the public in the late 1880s. Its 78 acres cost £120,000. It boasts what is believed to be one of the most beautiful gardens in Britain, 'The Old English garden'. This has shaded arbours, paths and luxuriant plantings. One part of it, the Shakespeare Garden, is said to have an example of every flower and herb mentioned in the bard's writings.

Opposite below: St Matthews Church, Brixton 1899 (43574) This beautiful town church, with its imposing facade with massive Corinthian pillars, is at the corner of Brixton Hill and Effra Road. It was built as one of four commemorative churches by Parliament as a thanksgiving for victories at Waterloo.

CLAPHAM is a long straggling suburb set along the busy high road that runs south from Stockwell towards rural Surrey. It is dominated by a huge expanse of common with a bandstand and ponds. Grouped around are grand villas built for wealthy London bankers and businessmen, who enjoyed the sensation of having a flavour of the great outdoors outside their city homes.

Right: St Barnabas Church, Clapham 1899 (43586)

Below: The Railway Junction, Clapham 1899 (44026) Before the coming of the railway in 1839, there was little to see here other than the Falcon Inn and a crossing of two lanes. As the various railway companies extended their networks further out into the suburbs, the single signal box was replaced with a busy station and a growing mesh of intersecting lines. Soon it grew into the most impressive and largest railway junction in the world.

Above: Clapham Common 1885
(C327217) An early photographer slides a
glass plate into his bulky brass camera,
while his two subjects stand stock-still and
stony-faced ready for the long exposure.
We must hope this photographer was
more honest than one or two of his
colleagues - many Victorians were not so
familiar with their appearance as we are
today. Some unscrupulous photographers
were known to have palmed off
unsuspecting sitters with spare prints of
other clients! Here the proud parents
show off the new addition to their family.

**Left: The Pond and Band Stand, Clapham
Common 1898** (42814) Bordered by trees
and sumptuous villas, the 220 acres of
Clapham Common have long been
popular with Londoners for Sunday
afternoon strolls. Yet the Common had
once been described as a 'desolate
morass'. Then public subscriptions
funded the creation of footpaths, ponds
and avenues of trees.

**Overleaf: The Roman Catholic Church,
Clapham 1899** (43591)

Right: The Common Pond, Tooting Bec 1898 (42797) This expansive open space was acquired for the public in the 1870s. The land was once a dependency of the Benedictine Abbey of St Mary of Bec in Normandy. By the beginning of Victoria's reign it had become a fashionable country retreat, and was bordered by broad avenues fringed with trees containing many imposing villas and mansions. Until late in the 17th century, ancient rights permitted local people to cut gorse and to dig gravel on the common. The Duke of Bedford, who owned much of the adjoining land, attempted to fence off the Common so that he could swell his own coffers through sales of the gorse. The riots that ensued quickly made him change his mind.

Above: The Pond, Thornton Heath c1890 (34372) It is said that the desolate wilds of Thornton Heath were the haunt of the highwayman, Dick Turpin. He would not have managed to escape for long if he had survived into the Victorian era. Here, the pond has been given a municpal make-over, with lavish plantings of shrubs and neat railings. On the right is the Plough & Harrow.

Top: Streatham 1898 (42778) A panoramic view from the Common. **Above: The High Road, Streatham 1898** (42785) Streatham's long High Road stretches from Brixton Hill in the north to Norbury in the south, a distance of two miles. The view shown here is little changed today, with the spire of St Leonard's church still soaring over the roof tops. In the centre, where the road divides, is an ornate Gothic-style water fountain. The High Road swings to the left here, and the tight neck of buildings on both sides gives way to the open Common. There is an alarmingly tall and wobbly ladder reaching high up to the roofs of the shops!

Above: On the Wandle at Beddington 1894 (34376) This tiny, meandering waterway provided the driving force for the wheels of 90 watermills! In the background is evidence of Beddington's own heritage of corn milling - there is an old mill wheel propped up against a house wall. Beddington's ancient mill, known since the 1800s as Lambert's Snuff Mill, is mentioned in Domesday. Small children dangle their legs over the rails of the bridge, watching their older brother shrimping with a net.

Left: The Female Orphanage, Beddington 1891 (27430) This imposing old building was the home of the Carew family for half a millennium. They finally moved out in 1859, when it was rebuilt as an orphanage. The magnificent Tudor hall, the orangery and red brick pigeon-house with nesting places for 1000 birds have all survived. The buildings are now in use as a school.

CARSHALTON. The great Victorian critic and social reformer, John Ruskin, believed there was no more beautiful riverside scenery in the south than that which borders the River Wandle. With its peaceful and placid pond, the surface dappled with the reflections of overhanging branches of majestic trees, Carshalton offers welcome sanctuary from the rush and pressure of London life.

Top: The Pond at Carshalton 1896 (37669) This perfect lake is one of the sources of the River Wandle. Ruskin had it cleared in memory of his mother, and set a stone here for travellers, asking that 'this well be kept sacred for the service of men's flocks and flowers and be by kindness called Margaret's Well'. **Above: The Church and Pond, Carshalton 1928** (80682) This fine church of flint and white stone rises over the waters, its copper spire gleaming in the sunlight. The white house known as Queen's Well was demolished in living memory. It is believed that the prefix 'Cars-' means watercress, which once grew in bright green hummocks in the clear waters.

Above: Parish Church, Carshalton 1928
(80693) Another view of this tranquil church and village. It is hard to believe that just a mile or so away is the massive housing estate of St Helier, begun by the London county Council in 1927 to house London's overflowing population.

Left: The Bridge at Hackbridge 1895
(35148) The railway to Sutton crosses the Wandle at Hackbridge. A pony and trap jogs along the dusty lane, its driver peering down dreamily into the babbling water. This stretch of the Wandle was once the site of many local trades, and of watermills producing gunpowder, wool, leather and snuff.

CROYDON has seen more changes in the past century than almost any other area of outer London. It was once a market town of 12,000 people, and before that in Tudor times the remote haunt of charcoal-burners. Its position on the great road from London to Brighton ensured it could not keep its antiquated character for ever. Yet it still nurses a few pockets of its heritage, notably the 16th-century Whitgift Hospital in North End. The entire borough boasts over 120 churches, chapels and mission halls!

Right: North End, Croydon 1896 (38651) This busy shopping thoroughfare leads from the High Street towards the railway station. A little way down on the right is J Lyons Tea House, the chain of early tea shops that encouraged the Victorian and Edwardian man in the street to dine out. Previously, this luxury had been the exclusive province of the well-to-do.

Above: High Street, Croydon 1900 (46111) Although it is now at the very heart of this huge conurbation, Croydon High Street was once little more than a bridle path across open fields. But Victorian engineers shrewdly took advantage of its position on high ground, and the old dusty street became a bustling thoroughfare linking London with Brighton and the south. It was widened in 1895. The brick building with decorative white stone quoins on the right is the Greyhound Restaurant and Tea Rooms.

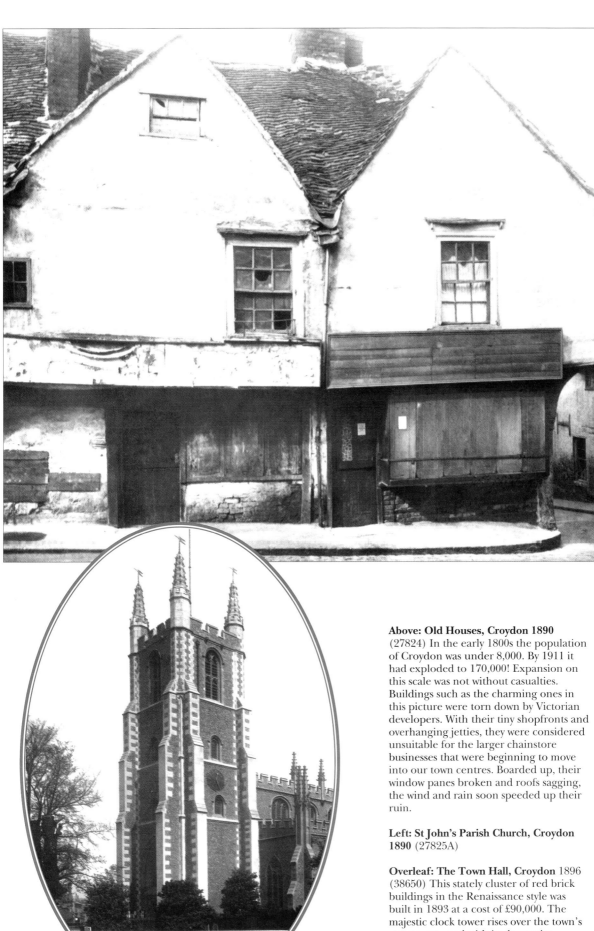

Above: Old Houses, Croydon 1890
(27824) In the early 1800s the population of Croydon was under 8,000. By 1911 it had exploded to 170,000! Expansion on this scale was not without casualties. Buildings such as the charming ones in this picture were torn down by Victorian developers. With their tiny shopfronts and overhanging jetties, they were considered unsuitable for the larger chainstore businesses that were beginning to move into our town centres. Boarded up, their window panes broken and roofs sagging, the wind and rain soon speeded up their ruin.

Left: St John's Parish Church, Croydon 1890 (27825A)

Overleaf: The Town Hall, Croydon 1896 (38650) This stately cluster of red brick buildings in the Renaissance style was built in 1893 at a cost of £90,000. The majestic clock tower rises over the town's streets, crowned with its decorative cupola. The ornate porch in the centre leads to the public library.

Top: North End, Croydon 1902 (48176) This busy scene shows the No 24 tram en route from Thornton Heath to Purley. On the right is Upson & Co, 'The Great Boot Provider' (the Edwardian shopkeeper was never slow to sing his own praises) and, next door, Andrews' Bazaar, where the local population could be sure of a good bargain. **Above: The Swan & Sugar Loaf 1899** (44181) This magnificent tour de force of Victorian pub design was erected in 1896. Here we see the old and the new modes of transport: a No 24 tram meets up with an old horse-drawn bus owned by Pratt Bros of Streatham.

SUTTON. If a Victorian inhabitant of Sutton were able to come back and look round his home town today he would probably be unable to recognise it. Like Croydon it has undergone huge changes. Set strategically on the old Reigate and Brighton road, Sutton was an important coaching stop for many years. Yet, with its parks and leafy side streets, it still offers some peace and quiet, and the sanctuary of the North Downs are just a few miles away.

Right: The Cock Hotel, Sutton 1890 (27423A) This historic old coaching inn was the first stage for a change of horses on the road to the south from London. Impatient regulars wait at the door for opening time, one resplendent in top hat and white scarf. On the left, a market trader stands by his display of bedding plants, which are neatly laid out in wooden trays.

Above: The Cock Hotel, Sutton 1898 (41708) The lovely old inn in the top photograph did not survive for long after the picture was taken. It was replaced by the grand Victorian extravaganza shown here. Devoid of local styling and materials, it typifies the Victorian monumental approach to public buildings. Nevertheless, it was a much-loved local landmark until it, too, was demolished in 1950, when the High Street was widened.

Above: High Street, Sutton 1932 (48865)
You can just see the The Cock Hotel sign
in the distance in the centre of the road.
We are at the upper end of the High
Street, looking north, close by the railway
station. The road takes a tumble from
here, dropping down through the busy
shopping centre, before rising once more
towards Rose Hill and Mitcham. It is a
street of classic Victorian shop buildings,
civic and dignified. Similar developments
were going up all over London.

**Left: The London & Provincial Bank,
Sutton 1900** (45478) Set on the opposite
corner from the Cock Hotel, this
imposing building typifies the style of
brash, new bank premises beloved of the
Victorian financiers. It peers down with
lordly magnificence on the smaller shops
alongside, and was doubtless designed to
impress - and intimidate - clients.

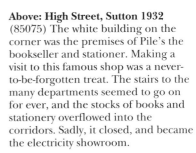

Above: High Street, Sutton 1932
(85075) The white building on the corner was the premises of Pile's the bookseller and stationer. Making a visit to this famous shop was a never-to-be-forgotten treat. The stairs to the many departments seemed to go on for ever, and the stocks of books and stationery overflowed into the corridors. Sadly, it closed, and became the electricity showroom.

Left: The County School, Sutton 1903
(50283) A quiet and leafy backstreet, away from the rush of traffic. Beyond the school is the Fire Station.

Opposite above: High Street, Sutton 1932 (85078) Stretching over the street is the old signboard of the Greyhound Inn. The inn is long gone, and this lower end of the High Street is now packed with chain stores.

Opposite below: The Angel Hotel, Sutton 1896 (38926) Another old inn, close by the Angel Bridge at the northern edge of the town.

Right: The Green, Wallington 1903 (49189) Once a remote hamlet with a thriving local herb industry, Wallington has grown swiftly into a populous green suburb between Sutton and Croydon, split by main roads. The broad green, with its elm trees, is a popular place to stand and idly watch the traffic flow by. Wallington once boasted what is believed to be the first railway in the world, the Surrey Iron Railway: in the early days of the 19th century horse-drawn wagons carried passengers from Wandsworth to Croydon.

Below: Manor Road, Wallington 1903 (49185) The Melbourne Hotel is on the corner on the right. You can see the original brick facade, roof and round-headed windows, behind. The landlord has extended his premises out onto the street, creating a classical-style entrance room. A man is sweeping the pavement gutter.

Above: The Red Lion Hotel, Coulsdon 1906 (57073) This old inn on the Brighton run was once host to 40 coaches a day. It was extended by the Victorians - you can see the old mansard roof behind. It has been replaced entirely in recent years by a mock Tudor half-timbered building.

Left: The Brighton Road, Coulsdon 1906 (57075) One famous guide book has said of Coulsdon that 'it knows the hubbub of the Brighton Road'. You would never guess it from the peacful Frith scene here. A nanny poses by a pram with a baby swaddled in white to ward off the hot sun. Apart from a few horse-droppings there is no evidence of any traffic whatsoever. Yet the peace had already been shattered by the coming of the car: in 1901, Edgar Crundy had thundered through and had been summonsed for driving too fast, his speed having been estimated by various witnesses at somewhere between 16 and 153 mph! The open and breezy chalk downs around Coulsdon have been relentlessly eaten into by new building.

URLEY. Tucked under the rim of the North Downs, Purley, like Coulsdon, was little more than a hamlet until late Victorian times. There were farms with sheep grazing the chalk hills, and only the clatter of horses' hooves to break the rural tranquillity. The railway changed its character for ever. People found they could work in London and still get back home for dinner in a place where you could enjoy the vision of hills through the dining room window.

Right: High Street, Purley 1903 (49445) Green & Sons' shop dominates this corner of the High Street, with its fine fascia signwriting, encouraging the local people to 'try our celebrated bread'. A medley of girls in floppy hats and pinafore dresses stare wistfully at the cakes on display in the window.

Above: Purley from the Hills 1903 (49438) Rank upon rank of new houses smother the valley. In the background the railway marches relentlessly on, over bridges and along embankments. Purley, like Coulsdon, is filling up with commuters who wish to return home from their desk-bound City jobs to enjoy a slice of the English countryside. **Opposite page: The Tram Terminus, Purley c1903** (49450)

CHEAM was conceived as the ultimate suburban rural village, with its uniform imitation half-timbered buildings, broad avenues and leafy crescents. It is fortunate to have Nonsuch Park so close by, which has helped preserve its atmosphere of countryside tranquillity. Yet it is only a couple of miles from its huge and populous neighbour, Sutton.

Right: The Old Cottage, Cheam 1925 (77066) This celebrated old timber-framed cottage is said to have been moved to make way for the majestic palace of Nonsuch, built by Henry VIII in the great park near by. Inside its tiny rooms were found coins and pots from the Roman era, and earthernware made locally during the era of the Black Death.

Below: The Railway Bridge, Cheam 1904 (51198)

Above: The Broadway, Cheam 1932
(85087) Sedate and cosy, Cheam is a
classic 20th-century half-timbered
confection. Even the gable windows of the
shops have leaded panes. Yet traffic
thundered through the Broadway en
route to North Cheam and Banstead in
living memory, until a bypass restored a
little of the planners' original utopian
dream. On the left, just beyond the tree,
is the Old Cottage shown on the previous
page.

Left: High Street, Cheam 1934 (86078)
This the road to Epsom. The shops soon
come to an end and the road makes a
sharp turn to the left by one of the gates
to Nonsuch Park, where Henry VIII had
his celebrated palace.

Top: The House, Nonsuch Park, Cheam 1904 (51196). Although it has an air of grandeur, this battlemented house bears no comparison to Henry VIII's celebrated palace which once stood here. **Above: Haymaking in Nonsuch Park, Cheam 1925** (77074) Mowing and pitching old-style, the wagon almost toppling over under its load. **Opposite: Nonsuch Park, Cheam 1904** (51197) The glory of Cheam are the 300 green acres of Nonsuch Park, where there are wide open spaces for walking and sheltered woodland glades for family picnics. A pony and trap follows the old ivy-covered wall of the garden. In the background are the roofs of the house.

Top: The Broadway, Fulham 1890 (F69001) A busy city scene, with a convoy of horse-drawn buses advertising Nestlés Chocolate and Hudson's Soaps. On the left is the Granville Theatre. Up a ladder, just beyond the glass entrance porch, a man is pasting up a new billboard. On the extreme left is an untidy pile of empty beer crates. **Above: Street Musicians in Putney c1900** (P332030) Street musicians were a popular diversion for the hordes of children who roamed the streets of London. Here a barrel organ grinds its way through a popular tune. There is also what looks to be a monkey in a cage.

KINGSTON UPON THAMES. This fine old Thames-side market town has an illustrious Royal heritage. In 838 AD Egbert held a Great Council here, and the town still treasures its celebrated Coronation Stone. At Kingston the Thames slides easily by, and once barges clustered around the wharves loading and unloading timber and other goods. Today the river is equally as busy, but now the boats that throng in the waters below the town bridge are there for pleasure alone.

Right: The Yacht Basin, Kingston 1906 (54719) A congestion of racing dinghies beat, tack and close haul to avoid each other. Favourably perched on the banks of the Thames, and with a fine many-arched bridge that was widened in 1914, Kingston has a strong attraction for idlers who enjoy messing about in boats. Jerome K Jerome began his eventful excursion up the Thames here.

Above: The Coronation Stone, Kingston 1893 (31767) King Edward the Elder was crowned here at Kingston in 900 AD, seated on the Coronation Stone that we see here. The town's regal associations were emphasised by the Victorians with the addition of the crown of ornate iron railings and stone pillars embellished with Romanesque decoration. It has since been moved to a quiet, shady spot near the Market Place. Behind it is a brewer's dray unloading barrels into the cellars of the Griffin Hotel.

Above: High Street, Kingston 1906
(54710) Here we are looking back
past the Griffin Hotel towards the
Coronation Stone.

**Left: The River Thames, Kingston
1890** (23552) Anglers and idlers gaze
out at the mesmerising water flowing
placidly by. Before the Victorian era
fishing had been a sport of the gentry,
yet it grew hugely in popularity during
the 19th century, as the working man
began to make the most of his hard-
won leisure time. In the background is
one of the flat-bottomed Thames
barges, which carried produce up and
down the river.

**Opposite top: Market Day, Kingston
1906** (54706) Stalls offering
everything from plants to dress fabrics
fill the broad space in front of the
handsome Market Hall, built in 1840.

**Opposite below: The Church,
Kingston 1906** (54715)

Above: Messenger's Boat House, Surbiton 1896 (38336) Two sprit-sail Thames sailing barges discharge opposite the famous boat house. The bargemen, one with his trousers hitched up with string and the other in waistcoat and battered bowler, have lifted the covers off the holds and are unloading a cargo of scrap iron onto a cart. The front barge is registered in Glasgow.

Left: The River from Queen's Promenade, Surbiton 1896 (38332) There was boundless fun to be had out on the open water. At weekends the river heaved with rowing boats and pleasure craft, and you could barely find space to dip the oars.

Opposite: The Water Splash, Kingston 1906 (54725) Mr Cornell the carrier's cart negotiates the flowing waters. In the background is J Batson's coach, cart and van building workshop.

Right: Queen's Promenade, Surbiton 1907
(58269) This flower and shrub-fringed
promenade made the perfect setting for a
peaceful afternoon stroll.

Below: Queen's Road, Surbition 1896
(38333) Jerome K Jerome has left us an
unforgettable account of life on the water
around Kingston. He began his journey up
the Thames (so hilariously recorded in *Three
Men in a Boat)* at Kingston Bridge just seven
years before this photograph was taken.
Sitting at the tiller, he would have soon
passed the spot we see here. He describes
the prospect: 'The glinting river with its
drifting barges, the wooded towpath, the
trim-kept villas on the other side, Harris, in
a red and orange blazer, grunting away at
the sculls ... all made a sunny picture, so
bright but calm, so full of life, and yet so
peaceful, that, early in the day though it was,
I felt myself being dreamily lulled off into a
musing fit.'

**Opposite page: St Raphael's Church,
Surbiton 1906** (54724A)

WICKENHAM. During the 17th and 18th centuries, Twickenham became a popular residential area, growing up around the fashionable and wealthy who built their homes along the riverbanks of the Thames. The original village grew outwards from around St Mary's Church and the Green as population increased dramatically, following the coming of the railway.

Right: Heath Street, Twickenham 1909 (T91001) Now resembling a busy town High Street, in Edwardian days this street was safe enough with so little traffic for dogs to wander about unrestrained. At the junction of the main roads through Twickenham, the rather imposing building in the centre of the photograph now houses a branch of one of the major banks.

Above: The Palm House, Kew Gardens 1899 (43756) Kew Gardens are a short distance down river from Twickenham, and were a very popular destination for Londoners' days out, until recently costing only a penny for entrance. The Palm House is another example of Victorian expertise in building glasshouses or conservatories: the exotic species cultivated therein would otherwise not withstand northern weather and could be kept at a temperate and moist climate.

Top: The Island, Twickenham 1890 (23535) The boathouse of a well-known local waterman, Charlie Shore (1858-1911) is to the left of this photograph, together with some of his boats. The boathouses to the right were destroyed during the Second World War.
Above: Queen's Head, Twickenham 1890 (23536A) The church of St Mary's stands close to the river: memorials to Alexander Pope and Thomas Twining, two illustrious past residents, are to be found there. The Queen's Head is more commonly known as The Barmy Arms, which bears a legend referring to a previous landlord's 'barminess'. The word is also a term for froth on top of fermenting ale.

RICHMOND. Originally known as Shene, Henry VII rebuilt the manor house in 1499 and called it Rychemonde after his Yorkshire earldom. A village prospered around the manor, which attained the status of a palace. Many moved to the country, as Richmond then was, to be away from the plague-infested city. Some fine early 18th-century architecture survives, described in detail by Dickens in *Great Expectations*. Disraeli visited Richmond in 1849 and was enchanted by Richmond Green.

Top: The Bridge, Richmond 1890 (23544) Increased population in the 18th century called for a bridge across the river, which could otherwise only be crossed by ferry. Completed in 1777 it is still one of the most graceful to cross the Thames. **Above: The Terrace, Richmond 1899** (43748) The houses of the Terrace mainly date from the 18th century. It is probable that Mrs Fitzherbert was living here when she first met her future husband, the Prince of Wales.

Above: Riverside, Richmond 1890
(23545) Boats are moored along the
riverbank: boating was a popular leisure
pursuit of the Victorians who loved to
spend their time on water. The towpath
along the river is still known as Riverside
and can be followed to Kew.

**Left: Star and Garter Hotel , Richmond
1899** (43743) The Star and Garter Hotel,
built in the 1870s, became a home for
wounded servicemen after the First
World War, and has been known as the
Royal Star and Garter Home for
Disabled Sailors, Soldiers and Airmen
ever since. Administered by a Board of
Governors appointed by the Red Cross, it
stands in a commanding position near
the gates of Richmond Park, on what is
now known as Star and Garter Hill.

**Overleaf: View from the Bridge,
Richmond 1899** (43739)

Above: On the Thames, Richmond 1899 (43742) Boating was a popular Victorian pastime: steam-launches were a superior form of transport compared to popular punts and rowing skiffs. The modern Richmond is the only London Borough with land on both sides of the Thames, including not only Richmond upon Thames but also Twickenham, Teddington, Barnes and the Hamptons.

Left: View from Richmond Hill, Richmond 1899 (43746) Richmond Hill looks down on a view described by James Thomson in 1727 as "a goodly prospect of hills, and dales, and woods, and lawn and spires and glittering towns and gilded streams."

Opposite above: Bridge, Teddington 1899 (43051) The suspension bridge shown carries a footbridge, passing above Teddington Weir, whose sluice-gates are the lowest in the river. The lock, first in ascent and last in descent of the Thames, was built in stone in 1859, with a small skiff lock alongside.

Opposite below: Lock and Rollers, Teddington 1899 (43054)

HAMPTON. The Saxon words describe the position of the first settlement here, 'the farm in the bend of the river'. The manor was acquired by the Knights Hospitaller in 1236 until Thomas Wolsey leased it in 1514, pulling down their manor house and building the palace that was then transformed and taken over by Henry VIII. A mile away upstream and downstream, Hampton and Hampton Wick gradually developed.

Right: Church, Hampton 1890 (23556) The church of St Mary's looks romantic in the distance, with willows trailing in the Thames. It would have been relatively new when this photograph was taken, as it was reopened in 1885, wtth a new chancel added in 1888.

Above: The Bridge, Hampton 1890 (27212) Clearly showing a bend in the river, Hampton was an old-fashioned village, straggling along the river bank, with willow trees and an island that was a favourite with anglers, and now a fixed mooring for houseboats, known as Tagg's Island.

Top: Hampton Court Palace 1899 (43044) One of the finest examples of Tudor architecture in Britain, this royal palace on the banks of the Thames was partially restored by Sir Christopher Wren. The gardens, arbours and hunting lodges made it a favourite with successive monarchs since the time of Henry VIII. Henry's presence, and that of his unfortunate wives, can still be felt today, but one attraction of surprising popularity is the vast medieval kitchen. Elizabeth I improved the gardens and held masques and banquets there. **Above: Hampton Court Palace 1899** (43046) and **Overleaf: On the River, Hampton Court 1896** (38341)

Index